The Knowledge Enterprise
Redefining Higher Education

The Knowledge Enterprise
Redefining Higher Education

C.R. Mitra
Parimal Mandke

SAMSKRITI

SAMSKṚITI
C-9020, Vasant Kunj, New Delhi-110070

ISBN 81-87374-27-6

Typeset by Vaibhav Graphics, New Delhi
Printed at Shivam Offset, New Delhi
Published by M. Sengupta for Saṁskṛiti, New Delhi-110070

Contents

Preface

This book was written to present a theory of Higher Education on which we have been working, on and off, for several years. During the same period, we were called upon to guide major renewal programs of different types of institutions of higher learning.

Although the sponsors of these institutions fully supported the programs, things were not easy. We discovered that on matters of Higher Education inherited norms, practices and habits preset thinking. On deeper analysis, it came as a revelation to us that in the name of educational theory, the strong viewpoints of social scientists and economists were pushed. These viewpoints are perfectly legitimate as far as they went. They were rightly valid for any institution or organization but they were necessarily not specific to institution of higher learning. This log jamming of thinking had to be broken. Our quest for a true theory of Higher Education thus began.

It is interesting that the ordinary description of a university is captured in the following words - Universities stand for development and distribution of knowledge. On further thought, without entering into more details, we decided to use this word knowledge as a metaphor and then fill in the details. All activities of a university, be that teaching-learning, creation of knowledge, or application of knowledge etc. etc. can and should be expressed in a new language and idiom around the word knowledge. Further reference could be made to Chapter 9. If we remain confined to only two activities: production of knowledge and knowledge in action, we can describe all details of one of the most complex organizations called a modern university.

Conceptually, as soon as the knowledge metaphor was born, we decided to work through new methods of problem solving in Higher Education. We chose to separate the philosophical issues from the intense involvement of practical affairs. Philosophy says what is ideal and desirable; science says what really is the reality, but engineering, first having established what is not impossible, transforms the endeavour towards achievement. Engineering approach appealed to us and the word "*knowledge engineering*" was coined accordingly. To meet demands of practical action, knowledge engineering needed to manipulate knowledge at the engineer's will. This was achieved by the objectification of knowledge where knowledge can be treated as a physical entity and can be pursued through the process in which knowledge is involved. Treated in this way, knowledge becomes independent of the properties of the environment and the vagaries of the process. Problem of measurement, which bothers all engineers, can now be handled with elegance.

It should be evident that we have been inspired by the method of reductionism-holism of modern science. In this fragmented form, we have defined the system through our knowledge metaphor. Next, we need another objective approach to describe the entire system.

Now, the mutuality of natural science and engineering science should be invoked. Natural science, through agreed methodology, described the phenomenal world. Engineering science, while accepting the description, must manipulate the world thus revealed. But it imitates the scientific process of constant effort to move from the specific to the general, small correlation to universal law. It was natural, therefore, for us to develop the Mitra Model (MM) to meet all practical necessity- analytical or synthesis of Higher Education. Our need was to find a model, which at once abstracts everything that went before and reveals everything that is likely to emerge in the future. MM is the logical presentation of all universities so far manifested and narrated in Chapter 6. It is as if all universities have coalesced into the logical model. Most interestingly, the logical model would become the template on which the reality has to be configurated as per the vision of the consultant and the requirement of the responsible provider (Chapters 3 and 5).

As our ideas evolved and matured, many things appeared natural to us. Institutions formed with care and high cost have been launched. But even though the design was perfect to make them socially acceptable, economically viable and approved by the market, they continued to be intellectual drags. It is evident to us that the sad situation happened because the epistemological issues were not faced. What perhaps could have been done is to first design the knowledge aspect of the design and then superimpose societal, economic and market issues on the tentative design.

If we had left the matter at this stage the exercise would have been merely rhetorical. On hindsight, it so appears that we were obliged to intuitively make basic educational alterations in the three institutions that we would mention later. At that time, these changes, even if they worked remained adhoc. While working in the new theory, we ensured that the network of intuited changes we had successfully implemented matched with the elementary structure of the theory. Compared to many other educational reformers, we were lucky to achieve three situational advantages, namely: (i) a coherent metaphor, idiom and language unique to Higher Education developed; (ii) the thinking in Higher Education can now be restored to its proper destiny in the epistemological sphere and (iii) the vital task of monitoring an existing institution and the design of a new institution is possible now from the fundamentals. There is no longer a necessity to merely extend the past. Higher Education is now part of a grand knowledge enterprise.

Before we close, it would be helpful if we describe how the book has been planned. Just as an idea and the networking of the ideas are complex, adequate description of what we wish to state becomes unmanageable. There were many fundamental thoughts, which had to be delineated before we would link up the thoughts in a sequential pattern. We were constantly faced with tautology and oxymoron. It was a veritable confusion. What we finally decided was to leave the matter to the reader.

The book broadly contains three parts. Part I is the central set of ideas and expositions leading to the development of the theory and its applications. Part II contains chapters, which act as ideational means to Part I. Each chapter in Part II is self contained and stand-alone. But in the back of our mind, we kept the need for these chapters to also serve the purpose of chapters in Part I and Part III. On the other hand, Part III only touches on future vistas now revealed to us while the theory unfolds its logic. It is not merely an exercise in futurism; it is a challenge for practitioners to seize new opportunities now revealed through the tip of the iceberg.

Besides the three parts, we present for convenience of reading, a list of abbreviations, list of diagrams and a glossary.

Abbreviations

AR	Academic Regulations
DP	Degree Provider
D-W	Data/Information/Knowledge/Wisdom
EK	Expert Knowledge
HE	Higher Education
HEI	Higher Education Institution
K	Knowledge
Kf	Final Knowledge
KHK	Know-how Knowledge
Ki	Initial Knowledge
KWK	Know-what Knowledge
MM	Mitra Model
NDP	Non-degree Provider
POS	Program of Studies
S&T	Science & Technology
WOS	World of Studies
WOW	World of Work
ΔK	Knowledge Gained
ΔT	Flow of Time

List of Diagrams

Part I: Fundamentals

Wherein an attempt has been made to invent the knowledge metaphor to fully characterize Higher Education.

1

Higher Education and the Human Condition

(a) General Observations

- Literacy and education are must for a cohesive society. Without a proper level of input of these items, communication between the members of society would snap. Some pronounce them as important as food, shelter, health, etc.
- As in health, literacy and education both can easily relapse to a lower level. Thus, means have to be formally introduced to maintain the quality of all education and training.
- Higher Education can simply be taken as that level of education, which is in the post-secondary stage. At this stage, we do not need to distinguish between academic and vocational aspects of human development. We are concerned with practical means of ensuring mental achievement and related skills.
- Higher Education can easily be seen to serve the custodial responsibility of all education. This further accentuates the intimate relationship between Higher Education and the human spirit.
- When we focus on university education, it would be worthwhile to recall how the university came into existence even from ancient times and well into the medieval days and how university education was made an organized form of training professionals. Thus, it is clear that furtherance and advancement of knowledge and proper preparation of a person for a vocation seems to become unavoidable responsibilities of a university for all times.
- No doubt, the aspiring needs of a society have turned to the universities to participate in many more ramifications of the two primary historic responsibilities mentioned in Chapter 9.

(b) Impact of Higher Education

It would be helpful to recall some historic events affecting Higher Education and hence the human condition (Chapter 6):

(i) On the professions — This incidental association between a vocational training and fundamentals of knowledge has rendered vital service to every profession. They have become stronger and more creative. This is the mantle of engineering science we have referred to earlier and would have occasion to use it subsequently.

(ii) On University mission itself — The thrust Berlin University gave to research as part of the curriculum became exemplary. American universities through land grant system enlarged and diversified the idea. The well-known graduate schools have come into existence in competition with professional schools. Intellectual eminence of basic science with applied engineering is now firmly established.

(iii) On minds of people — London University and in some form, both Oxford and Cambridge furthered the cause of the first globalization that colonial England pushed through the world. It is interesting but for the establishment of the first three universities in India (Kolkata, Mumbai and Chennai) the spread of rational thought would have been more difficult.

(iv) On productivity and skill formation — Armed services training, extension work in agriculture, superior skill formation through universities arranged workshop, etc.

(v) On social reforms — Women's colleges aiming towards social equality.

(c) Some Correlations

It is not suggested, in the absence of research with a new direction, that cause-effect relationship can be clearly pronounced everywhere. Nevertheless, we list below following combination of terms to indicate some correlations, even though imprecise.

- Rise of middle class and state of Higher Education.
- Post graduate education and hi-tech knowledge industry.
- Rapid growth of service industry and expansion of Higher

Education in both knowledge involvement and modern skill formations.

- Pressure for admission and social investment in Higher Education.
- Reputation of Higher Education Institution and export of Higher Education.
- Participation rate and spread effect of knowledge through students.

(d) The Future

- If Higher Education is so vital for the mental and material upliftment of every society, there should be a natural and persistent demand for more and more Higher Education Institutions. We are disturbed that this matter is expressed almost invariably in terms of supply and demand. Arguments get fragmented in terms of money, authority, regulation, control, etc. In order to make a debate out of this encounter, fundamental theories are invoked. Invariably theories of social development, economic laws and market forces amalgamate into a cacophony of noise. Forgotten is the fact that Higher Education is essentially a matter of dealing with knowledge and help the adherents become more knowledgeable.

We have concluded that knowledge, as a metaphor should come in all our discussion on university education or Higher Education. We shall describe the functioning and operation of Higher Education Institutions through the knowledge metaphor. There should be no mistake. Physical and administrative structure and financial need are vital. But in this case, they are vital because the citadel of knowledge itself is extremely important and crucial. We propose to relate all mundane and sundry items through the habits of a knowledge engineer who demands, seeks and establishes higher productivity of knowledge.

2

Knowledge in Action and Its Human Use

- Practical philosophers have said that knowledge without action has no value and action without knowledge is futile. We propose to paraphrase the statement to establish how knowledge without action is dormant just as a mineral resource or even human resource when not subjected to engineering operation remains outside our thought. Thus, the role of humans in this matter becomes a clinching issue. As knowledge engineers or knowledgists, we look forward to knowledge enhancing human enrichment.
- We have given two definitions to the word knowledge engineering in the Glossary.
- Before we are obliged to bring in more terms, let us for immediate purpose give two meanings to the same word knowledge :

  First - Awareness of the world (cognition), dormant, *know-what knowledge* (KWK). This is simply connotation associated with the content or state of the system.

  Second - Activity. A means to act more intelligently on the world. *Know-how Knowledge* (KHK). The domain of KHK, compared to KWK, is less definable and is more intuitive (tacit).
- Before we move into territory crisscrossed by streams of action caused by knowledge, we prefer to dispose off few matters where existing views seem to be very fixed and strong. Readers may detect it from Chapter 9 or through their own previous experience. Now to the factors.

Teaching-cum-Research

By imprecise usage, it is often forgotten that teaching at the university level is permanently tied up (inseparable bonds) with research and evaluation of the performance of the student. This may be called, *research of the first kind*.

Teaching is an upliftment of the knowledge endowment possessed by the student through transmission of knowledge through the intervention of teacher who possesses KWK and KHK. Now this process is so contextual that any moment, anywhere, in any institute, a self-respecting teacher is doing research on feedback mechanism to improve the text material. Even if KWK does not alter (because scientific growth has not added any new knowledge) KHK is constantly changing in each setting of teacher-student interaction. Thus, when people mention a need for updating the curriculum, our theory analyzes two distinct domains through two distinct processes of updating. A university may only have a teaching function to discharge, but it must do KHK research through a proper set up for institutional research. Such persons even if they do not do any other required research, must be full time teacher-scholars. This term is deliberately coined to distinguish from the well-known term research-scholar. To complete the discussion, it is important to record that most self-respecting universities include some more activities under the title of research than what would be covered in the role of teacher-scholar mentioned above. This additional obligation of a university may be called, *research of the second kind*. This activity is best described as normal or paradigmatic science or curiosity-oriented research. It becomes a required component of assignment of thesis for senior students.

Mission-oriented research is mostly the agenda of research sponsored by specialized agencies as a part of growth of Big Science. Fund-conscious universities encourage faculty to do this and receive handsome overheads from the sponsors. As in anything, there are contrary views entertained by scholars.

- The very first recorded interaction between *Guru* and *Shishya* offered a continuous on-line feedback to *Guru*. To some educators, teaching and evaluation is a unity of function. There is a movement very vigorously upheld to go for continuous and internal evaluation. One could easily agree that this activity would require systematic research for the sake of betterment of education.

- Against the above background, we come back to our main theme of knowledge in action. Knowledge certainly is an important indispensable tool to make the human being more intelligent. It is our contention that proper combination of human beings and knowledge will convert the educational and related processes more useful from the point of view of knowledge deployed.
- The new terms that we introduce on the basis of our exposition can convey a better meaning if we take advantage of associated processes. For example, in the domain of large production we have two kinds, namely, manufacturing industry and service industry. When knowledge became an important item for discussion, sometimes Higher Education has been categorized as a service industry. We do not recommend this action because of the inherent power of knowledge. We have suggested in this book the term knowledge industry as the third category. Manufacturing is fully regimented and is predictable. Service is too amorphous to allow proper prediction. But knowledge industry is based on intellectual foundation and as such is logically predictable.
- Now we turn to take stock of the territory assigned to knowledge in action. In Chapter 9, we have reported streams of knowledge in action. These have been prompted from conventions reported in literature and outcome of our previous book, *S&T in Action*. Since our focus is on university education, we would delineate only that portion of the territory to take up knowledge in action in the transmission stream. What we propose to do in Chapter 3, is a limited use of systems approach in the delineation of the territory on transmission of knowledge would be useful.
- Our theory generalizes the phenomena called knowledge in transmission.

There is a starting point from where the donor or sender ensures that the knowledge is sent out. Likewise, there is a terminal point where the beneficiary or receiver is located. Our theory certainly permits such a process of transmission of knowledge from sender to a receiver through a process, which can be designed.

We can immediately detect that the proposition is where the sender is the teacher and the receiver is the student. This generalized statement is correct as long as we amplify it in respect of matters other than the core knowledge issue. To be able to do justice to its responsibility, to defend its verdict on student performance and to ensure that the degree award is acceptable to both the World of Studies (WOS) and World of Work (WOW) the institution must fulfil the following conditions:

(i) entering student must fulfil prior academic requirement set by the institution.
(ii) the credential awarded by the institution must be continuously showcased to the peer group.
(iii) all rules and regulations must be transparent, uncomplicated and implementable.

- It can be seen that these restrictions are only imposed in a situation where degree is pursued. In the event, the certification issue is not a delicate factor; transmission can be handled as any transaction in the civil society. Imagine that the second outpost manned by the receiver does not need a credential or what is transmitted is a CBT, being sold by the sender, all the complicated academic structure that we have to build up would not be necessary. But in that case, the organization ceases to be a university.
- In the next chapter a full-fledged university system will be described in the knowledge metaphor using the logical model.

3

Theory Formulation and Elaboration

We visualize a Higher Education Institution (HEI) as a unique knowledge organization. This fact is also acknowledged by society, which gives only to the university special responsibilities. So far, we have developed a coherent vocabulary to deal with knowledge organization. What we now need is theoretical abstraction of any university in the knowledge metaphor. We have captured some essence of this idea in Chapter 6. Here we have identified core concepts and widely permissible practice consistent with the core concepts. What we need now is to develop a model, which is a logical model to subsume any real model, past, present or future. The logical model that we have used extensively is presented in a diagrammatic form under the heading, Features of the Mitra Model (MM).

The particular emphasis we gave to our quest for theory put us in a challenging situation. This is because it simultaneously tackled new conceptual issues and the challenge of quantification. We felt if the second part was not done, knowledge engineering details would not become evident to a chance reader.

We discovered it useful to repeatedly revisit and redefine items in the ideation of chapters in Part II. These chapters were not ever intended to be chronological. We needed to understand on a continuing basis the meaning of any vital component as well as the relationship between the components. We could easily see that the relationship in academic matters is very similar to a geodesic pattern. Dedicated to engineering approach, we discovered that much more than a mere statement of knowledge engineering was demanded. We looked for the objectification or quantification of knowledge very kindly. In fact, what we ultimately would have needed was a model of Higher Education. This model had to be a logical model, which is free from the situational features of the system or the environment. In short, we sought a formula or an equation. Much earlier, we had used the Mitra Model for a limited purpose to examine particularly input/output/black box situation.

(a) Mitra Model

We persevered and arrived at the following mathematical model.

In time-flow ΔT

$kf - ki = \Delta k$

(final knowledge – initial knowledge = knowledge flow)

Δk = POS, where POS is Program of Studies

$POS = \Sigma Dn^{I} + \Sigma Dn^{II} + \Sigma Dn^{III} + \ldots\ldots\ldots\ldots$

where Dn^{I}, Dn^{II} Dn^{III} are various disciplines of knowledge

System functions on the driving force supplied through the Expert Knowledge (EK) possessed by the teacher:

$$EK = KWK + KHK$$

System efficiency is described in an unusual way of knowledge consumption and knowledge investment (Chapter 8). Consistent with the stand, the estimates are made by focussing on the five items, namely, ΔT, Δk, POS, EK and Academic Regulations (AR) in Diagram 3.1.

The formula is really part of an endless chain, which we are examining for the moment. Just as ki is a product from another HEI, kf of our institution under consideration may very well be the input for still another HEI. It is significant that prescribed requirement of kf is that it must be acceptable to both WOS and WOW, in short, the very educational market. We could go on to dilate upon novelty on utilization of time and method that this formula can suggest to an alert designer. We propose to now present graphically the features of the Mitra Model in Diagram 3.1.

(b) Some Concluding Observations

For a large system, it is expected that there will be marginal variations anywhere in the Diagram, which should therefore not be taken, as uniquely determined and inflexible. Attention may be drawn to the following:

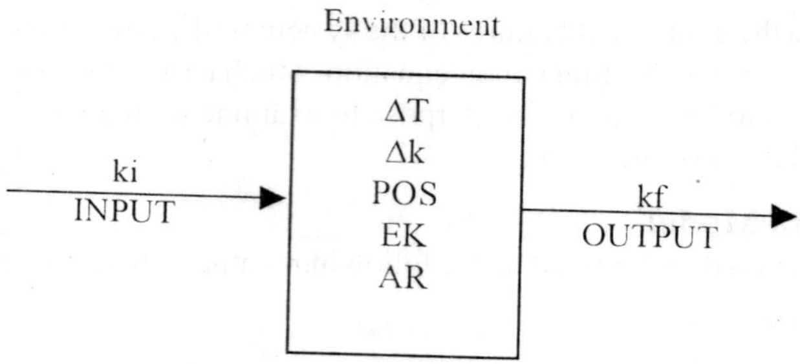

Features at the input Entitlement	Features of the black box	Features at the out-put Empowerment
• Eligibility for admission - ki • Performance in the previous level • Admission	• Program of Studies (POS) • Curriculum • Atomization of knowledge in terms of courses • Relationship bet-ween ki and kf • Interrelationship between courses • Academic architecture • Academic Regula-tions • KWK and KHK • Text-books-Course-ware • Teacher-Student • Mode of delivery • Credits • Environment • Internal environment needing constant resolution	• Certification/ Credential • Degree/ Diploma • Graduation • Third party validation by: - Govt. - Industry - Market - Accreditation Agency, etc. • Peer group rating of educational market consisting of WOS and WOW.

Diagram 3.1 : Features of the Mitra Model

(i) Variations at the input, ki

The arriving student may be more than ki or less than ki. Without harming the standard of the kf, HEI is prone to make admission with advance standing or with marginal deficiency, as the case may be.

(ii) Variations at the output, kf

Granted that the ultimate test is educational market, but there is always a departure for innovators. Just as in industry, in science and technology, we are familiar with new products, innovating universities do come forward with new kf and make it acceptable by the market.

(iii) Variations in the system

The basic concept of prior preparation or pre-requisite is the guiding requirement to allow: controlled variations in overloading or underloading, controlled variations in combination of courses to permit individualized career goals, etc.

Ideally, the institution must learn to do the chaos management. In reality, institutions are developing the method of dealing with operational specialization as much as they are keen on doing discipline specialization.

That the modern university demands from its teachers a self-developed competence in know-how knowledge generation is not always appreciated. In the high visibility of modern subject matters of KWK, we are likely to miss its unique contribution by teachers in universities.

4

Testing the Theory

- The theory is an attempt to do full justice to the epistemological aspects of Higher Education. It is a departure from the much-practiced discussions on Higher Education based on the principles of social science and economic science.
- Obviously, the testing of the theory should be done with equal adherence to originality. We meticulously tried to introduce innovations as described below :
  (i) Instead of proposing parameters of efficiency in conventional terms, we have developed epistemological indicators. For example, while dealing with knowledge in action, we should like to probe what is the maximum output from this action. Since knowledge is a sovereign entity, one must be prepared to develop the parameter to anticipate multiplying factors. In the absence of any suitable expression, we make do with the word 'productivity' of knowledge. Thus our theory should be able to measure the productivity of knowledge when confronted with alternate suggestions of techniques and institutions. We maintain that this is a vital contribution which liberates us from the perpetual habit of taking recourse to social science and economic principles alone.
  (ii) In the formulation and elaboration of the theory, we have taken full advantage of our experience. This experience is a cumulation of participation and study of three institutions of Higher Education. This is not the occasion to burden the reader with detailed case studies of these three institutions, where we were instrumental in implementing innovative solutions towards self-recovery of all the three. Let us call them A, B and C.

Institute A had a problem of implementing competitive admission policy. Institute B was a major recipient for self-reliant methodology for implementing the ideas donated by a foreign partner institution (Chapter 16.c). Institution C (Chapter 6) was not even a degree giver. Its need to provide access to degrees was established through the principle of parity with some foreign universities.

What is germane to the discussion at this stage is that for every problem, singly or collectively, we gave design solutions, which worked. On deep hindsight, we concluded that the intuited design presents elements of a knowledge theory in Higher Education. We equally came to another conclusion that a rare harmony is possible through responsible balancing of epistemological, societal and economic factors affecting the health of Higher Education. Thus our theory is not merely an outcome of fanciful thinking that needs to be tested. In fact, we kept on testing on-line as we were developing the theory for practical use. In the next chapter, we will dilate further on the application of the theory in institutional design, in institutional operations and in garnering vital principles in all institutional matters.

5

Applications of the Theory

It is necessary to demonstrate improvement on present practices in Higher Education, when it is trapped in a preset mode of thinking and doing. Our theory can apply from first principles on all-important matters demanding answers. The theory enables each informed person to find solutions, which are not necessarily, a mindless copy of another set up. Fundamentally, we initiate the principle that all solutions are valid and consistent. This is the hint we have given in Chapter 6.

(a) Design of New Institutions

Institutional design is the name we give to a process, which helps us in identifying vital details of proposed educational institution so that the future can be planned wisely.

However, design is a much-neglected area of interest on the part of educators. May be, the fact that Higher Education is widely subsidized from public funds has not induced rational thinking which would have been invoked if private contribution proportionately increased.

There is still another problem. There is no coherent theory of Higher Education acknowledging its basic role, namely, the development and distribution of knowledge.

We take advantage of the approach of knowledge engineering. We have in the Mitra Model captured a logical model representing any physical model mentioned in Chapter 6. Therefore, to create a new physical entity all that one has to do is to go back to Chapter 3 and start supplying details visualized in the Mitra Model. Actually, we are going back to basics and prudently run through the steps the following algorithm prescribes. It is the well-known procedure that a manual demands in the book of knowledge engineering.

Algorithm

(i) Avoid the normative process when the past is perpetuated by using norms of actual practices without referring to the context. The institute you want to design may never surface because you used inappropriate norms.

(ii) The first task is to know your bearing in the world of universities captured in literature, detailing both academic and non-academic features. Chapter 6 will help you narrow down the task. You need to pick one institution of your choice. The criteria of choice is entirely yours.

(iii) After you make your choice, subject it to a scrutiny through the guidance provided by Mitra Model, you should be now able to give more features of your choice, which are still tentative.

(iv) Now it would be the right occasion to verify your tentative choice against the norms applied so frequently by educators.

(v) There are bound to be differences between these three versions, namely, your informed choice, presumptions of the Mitra Model and the norms sanctified by an educational bureaucracy (government or private).

(vi) Obviously, this is not a simple process, but Higher Education is a serious matter for a society and votaries of Higher Education must train themselves into this art of institutional design.

(vii) Remember that Mitra Model is open-ended. There can always be more than one answer to the same questions. You should push the ideational effort (Part II) to focus on a bunch of solutions. This is the well-known problem-solving method of systems approach.

(viii) Now differentiate between solutions in the bunch by interjecting a novelty or a distinguishing unique feature. You wish to enter in a friendly competition amongst your peer group, who will have some views on the kf that you aim for. Thus, you will arrive at an academic orchestration which is characteristic of your institutional choice. This completes the academic design. This should always be done first before spelling out non-academic details. In fact, it is dysfunctional to name the human and material resources and then look for academic tasks these resources must discharge.

(ix) There are still further iterative actions to be painfully done if the academic program is discovered to be unsupported by social habit or economic feasibility. You have to do the entire design once more to create a harmonious blending of the three factors, namely, epistemological, societal and economic. We suspect and welcome that it can never be resolved. It is after all, a social judgement to pronounce what we expect from Higher Education. Armed with this information, it is for educational consultants to respond. They will have to articulate their response through Concept Papers, Feasibility Studies and Implementation Plans.

(b) Renewal/Recovery of Existing Institutions

The task envisaged here is application of the theory on an existing institution rather than setting up of a new institution. Thus, the methodology and the approach are basically trouble shooting. In various places in the book, we have done just that without making it obvious. What we therefore propose to do is to take a few items as below and draw the readers' attention on the issue discussed in different chapters in the book.

(i) Fear that modern market economy will adversely affect the epistemological responsibility of Higher Education (Chapter 3).

(ii) Anxiety that a subsidized system like Higher Education is inefficient and a dose of corporate management is required (Chapter 6).

(iii) Profit making is prohibited in the operation of Higher Education (Chapter 6).

(iv) If the student is a customer, what is his protection (Chapter 13)?

(v) Indulgence in research along with teaching should not be permitted to all Higher Education Institutions (Chapter 9).

(vi) Tie-up between institutions across the globe (Chapter 15).

(vii) Complaint that Higher Education Institution is

constitutionally incapable of timely updating its curriculum (Chapter 9).

(viii) Advent of Internet technology makes some people bold enough to suggest that teachers role can be eliminated (Chapter 12).

(ix) Funding should be sole responsibility of the government in power (Chapter 11).

(c) Enumeration of Principles of Knowledge Engineering

While elaborating concepts underlying knowledge engineering, we have been able to collect a set of principles, which are of great practical help to the end-user. We believe that along with the theory, these principles will be the basis for further intelligent decision making by educational institutions. Now to the enumeration of the principles.

(i) Demand for Higher Education will always escalate. The supply position is stretchable because the technology of delivery is not a specific mode as in the case of manufacturing.

(ii) Constant atomization of knowledge takes place in Higher Education. There is simultaneously a tendency to regroup knowledge prompted by the nature of end-use.

(iii) In discharging its responsibility in the awarding of degrees, Higher Education must work out an epistemological linkage between ki, kf and Δk.

(iv) However, in the commodification of knowledge Higher Education acts almost like a monopoly. Higher Education markets its own product through its own way. It is important to recall earnings made through research output, information output, consultancy, community service, etc., are not profits to be given to share holders.

(v) While meeting the requirements of awarding degrees, Higher Education invented the four-tier system as part of a cultural credential. While each tier stands alone, they are all networked by the very dynamism of knowledge.

(vi) No Higher Education Institution can avoid research of the first kind as a corollary to teaching.

(vii) Thus, the tendency is to use this seedbed for participating in a variety of directed researches whether through curricular need or sponsored research funded by outside agencies.

(viii) By its very nature, as a universal activity, it can work out global role.

(ix) Higher Education is a unique and unusual institution. It has outlasted anything else set up by man. The method adopted by Higher Education to perpetuate itself is worthy of emulation by most hyped organizations not excluding business.

Part II: Integrated Themes

Wherein we offer grand generalizations on some fundamentals to assist the development of our theory. It is through these generalizations in each chapter that we detect in its full scope of what we call Higher Education.

6

Higher Education as Shaped by History

- This is not a history of Higher Education. It is a probe on how Higher Education has fared in history, what has changed and what is unchanging.
- Let us recall from hoary past the *Guru-Shishya* (teacher-taught) setting for learning. It was followed by verdict of pupil performance through formal certifications.
- Somewhat later, simultaneously, scholars bonded together to advance frontiers of knowledge. Findings of research were published. Investigations were objective as in modern science.
- Above two coalesced. Many advantages accrued:
  - Unique and specialized institutions emerged.
  - Knowledge transmission for knowledge seekers enrolled as seekers of formal certification (degrees) reinforced knowledge generation.
  - Transparency and objectivity were secured by convention of printing of text book and research papers.
  - Teacher-scholar and research-scholar are no longer in separate compartments. Textbook writing became a form of research. Higher Education was inseparably tied to the teacher's active participation. Even the student asymptotically equals the teacher's knowledge endowment. Students are senior pupils. A student is an understudy to a professional knowledge worker. This gives rise to an interesting knowledge hierarchy in Higher Education (Chapter 10).
  - Higher Education is not part of free and compulsory need of a society as primary education is.

- Features and functions of Higher Education Institutions need fresh and tender study.

- First universities were born in India. These were set up for training of Buddhist priests and scholars. Intellectually they were not subservient to the temporal power. Objective was to serve a priestly professional class. Free thinking scholars who had reservations on Brahminical Hinduism flocked to these Universities from the known world.
- Much later, after a gap of centuries, a series of new universities cropped up in mediaeval Europe. These were meant for also the professions like medicine, law etc., in addition to priesthood.
- The European model spread to the colonies — new and old. The American version has some radically different features, which are spreading in preference to the European model.
- It is of interest to know how universities as Institutions survived over thousands of years, in thousands of form, in all parts of the globe. No man-made institution has survived this long, that too in a consistent form.
- All universities remained steadfast to the idea at its genesis. Ideas were transplanted but the form was local. Thus in giving expression to the concept, a complete permissiveness prevailed.
- Granted, it was a total randomness. But it was not a blind chance. Each institution had the same goal or destination. It would be illuminating to discover the pattern, which is dormant. A glimpse or even a hint of the pattern will facilitate further investigation intended in the book.

We avoid trite differentiation between institutions often reported in the literature, like Liberal Arts College, Engineering Universities, Campus-based Universities, Distance Learning Universities, etc. etc. Instead, we find it more fruitful to differentiate universities on the operational role they play, the epistemological responsibility they discharge and, above all, the joint efforts their teachers and students make to advance prestige of a Higher Education Institution. They happen to be post secondary and approved as Educational Institutions by Government.

(a) The Proposed Classification

(i) Teacher-intervening University

- most prevalent.
- universally endorsed by society, parents, students, etc.
- without this, there is a feeling of incompleteness in education.
- nothing can replace this in a normal sequential unfolding of delivery of education.

(ii) Teacher Non-intervening University

There are vital differences within themselves. The direct contact can be anywhere from close to zero to substantial. However, it cannot become zero whether or not technology is massively employed (Chapter 12).

(i) Examining only University (Not teaching).
(ii) Correspondence school type University.
(iii) Classical British Open University.
(iv) Various versions of (iii) above, such as Universities delivering education electronically.

At this stage, it is important to acknowledge that a large number of new institutions, operating in post secondary zone have cropped up. To avoid confusion, we categorize these as a part of a mixed bag as below.

(iii) A Mixed Bag

Pretenders, kibitzers, profit making training and coaching industry, corporate universities, etc.

- They are all non-University Institutions.
- Govt. does not recognize them as educational institutions.
- Some of them claim to use the university as a bench mark for inspiration or guidance.

Let us call them NDP (non-degree provider) (Institution C, Chapter 4). It is because of this claim they need to be studied historically and contemporarily.

(i) Non-degree providers have long past enjoyed informal acceptance as strong as degree providers.
(ii) It has to be also admitted that professional courses remained

outside university for a long time.

(iii) In the national or global interest, intersection between Higher Education Institutions must be encouraged, non-degree provider-degree provider, degree-provider-degree provider, non-degree provider-non-degree provider.

(b) Some Vital Conclusions

Recognizing that there is a substantial area of confusion on the fundamental features of Higher Education Institution, it is necessary to reiterate the following points again:

(1) The idea of a university is time honoured and also not negotiable (Refer to the mandatory requirements in Chapter 3).

(2) While variations are permissible, it does not mean that a model can be hoisted which is proposed to be operated without the expert knowledge of a teacher (Refer to KHK in Chapter 9).

(3) The classification offered here includes all Higher Education Institutions in time and space.

(4) It would be informative as well as educative if we could capture the essential structure of systems of Higher Education as well as their organizational features. For convenience, we confine ourselves to British, American and Indian systems (Tables 6.1 and 6.2).

(c) Fundamental Observation

- American Research University has come of age as a unique model to create knowledge capital of a society.
- In the thrust of R&D it has replaced the 19th century American industry sponsored R&D division.

Table 6.1

Three Systems Compared

Degree	Level	Features
I. American System (4-Tier)		
Ph.D.	Graduate School	* Academic hierarchy for each discipline
MS (1 year)		* Vertical movement of students
BS (4 year)	Undergraduate School	* Lines of divide pronounced
AS (2 year)	Junior Colleges	* *modus operandi* of Research University
II. British System (2 layers)		
		* Main destination is Bachelors in each discipline as well as general studies
Ph.D.		* Masters in each discipline is not sought after by students
Master (2 year)		
Bachelors (3 years)		* Conversion Bachelors treated under banner "Masters"
		* No defined Graduate School
III. Indian System (Multi-layer)		
		* Graduation = any Bachelors
Ph.D.		* Post-graduation = any Masters
		* Non-standardization of Bachelors
Masters		
Bachelors		* Masters created by clubbing inputs of both bachelors and Masters.

Table 6.2

A rough sketch of organization features

	Types	Top Management Name and Nature	Middle Level Knowledge Workers
(1)	Typical Business	- Board of Directors - Self perpetuating - CEO supremacy - Share holders	- Supine and repla-ceable - Nomenclature is unique
(2)	Proprietary College (Knowledge Business)	- Board of Directors - Self perpetuating - CEO supremacy - Share holders	- Supine and repla- - ceable - Nomenclature is tentative and changeable
(3)	American Research University	- Board of Trustees - Self-perpetuating - President supremacy - Stake holders	- Tenure, not pliable. Not replaceable - Nomenclature is unique - Recognition from outside - Performance evaluated by external peer group
(4)	A typical IIT	- Board of Governors - Self perpetuating - Chairman and not - Director's supremacy - No owner	- Permanent and not replaceable - Goals are academic - Differs from Indian University in form and not in substance - Performance evalu-ated by exclusive theory

(5)	A typical Indian University	- Executive Council - Self-perpetuating with lay public - participation - Dffused authority between Chancellor, Vice-chancellor and Government - No owner	- Permanent and perpetuating tends to unionize - Performance evaluated on bureaucratic terms

7

Emergence of the Institutional Form

Elsewhere we have observed that the nodal setting of a teacher and a student can spontaneously occur without a planned external inducement. This is all for the good of the teaching-learning process. It is now established that there are rules according to which the nodal setting is overcome by the institutional form. It is to be clarified that the institutional form is by definition opposite of autonomous form of learning. But the nodal unit here is very much part of the institutional form.

We now examine the circumstances, which induce the emergence of the institutional form. They are:

(i) Whenever a buyer and a seller use the open market to transact business, a transaction cost is involved. If the transaction cost exceeds the cost of setting up and operating an institution, it makes sense to start a new organization.

(ii) If the supply demand gap in education becomes uncomfortably large; creating a new institution may be strongly indicated.

(iii) Whenever the program of studies spans more disciplines than it is possible for a single teacher to do justice to the task, the institution ceases to be monochromatic. It is almost a new institution that emerges.

Promoter's Folly

We conclude by identifying some prescribed precautions the promoter of higher education must take in view of the rules stated above. These are:

(i) These rules prepare us for emergence of the institutional form. The same rules can equally reverse the process leading to institutional disintegration. Outsourcing, tie-ups, mergers, etc., can often prove to be dysfunctional.

(ii) The tuition fees are so arbitrarily fixed that the conditions of operationality of these rules are badly distorted. Either they are made very low through subsidization; or they are made very high because the buyer is persuaded to pay. Either case, the price is not at all related to the cost, which is a measure of the knowledge value one is dealing with. Only if the true market forces were allowed to operate, the instructive value of knowledge would have been revealed. The motto that some amount of subsidy is warranted in Higher Education and also that those who can pay must do so, should not lead civil societies to do irreparable damage to knowledge institutions. The matter is squarely in the epistemological domain.

8

Teachers as Stake-holders

- If a university primarily exists to develop and distribute knowledge (k), those who make a lifelong career in these functions of k should have the highest stake in the system. Unfortunately, the import of this statement is completely missed by some providers of Higher Education and also by a large number of teachers themselves. On the contrary, they view the teacher's role not as a k activist, but as merely an instrument of delivering lectures, of conducting tutorials and of evaluating answer books. Once the epistemological role of teachers is dismissed, it is so comfortable to subscribe to a syndrome as described below:
  (i) Teacher-propelled education and Technology-propelled education are one and the same thing.
  (ii) Scholarly textbooks can be replaced by multimedia-assisted courseware.
  (iii) Thus, technical hands can achieve much of the monitoring task. High-salaried teachers need not be hired.
  (iv) System will achieve efficiency, not available hitherto.

- The advocates of the syndrome evidently fail to appreciate some fundamentals listed below:

  (i) HE is familiar with technological changes, much often as an originator. If it is immersed in the "talk and chalk", this is because that is the most appropriate technology for the purpose. Historically, HE has hastened to adopt a technology, which increases the reach of educational coverage. Technology *ipso facto* does not improve the transmission process in the cognitive matter.
  (ii) Claims of better efficiency are an illusion. The situation, as

advocated, amounts to a come down on the D–W Continuum (Chapter 9) from k to information. Hence, claim can be valid only for information supply and not for k transmission.

(iii) The missing link is the teacher who with the prescribed Expert Knowledge (EK) will ensure the knowledge task in Higher Education. In the fulfilment of this task one naturally seeks the greatest efficiency.

- We will now develop a theoretical construct, which probes deeper how the teachers collectively uphold the system. A cross-reference to Chapters 3 and 9 is advisable.
- In the Diagram 8.1 the triangular area is the field where the teacher operates. MM stands for the universal theory, which guides his action. KWK captures the current thinking on the curriculum. KHK is the mirror of the stock of knowledge the teacher has already developed before meeting the class to deliver KWK.
- It is to note that KHK is not a prescribed requirement. Each teacher develops it as and when prompted by self-motivation. KHK is a perpetual source of academic administrators and such other knowledge-generalists.
- The prescribed qualifications of each teacher are stated in terms of KWK in whichever discipline of knowledge through named degrees. It is of interest to note that the profile of knowledge workers is universally stated in terms of unique degree a university awards. It also serves as job filters by all employers – universities, business, government, R&D Institutes, etc. When pressed, employers estimate a rough proportion between MM, KWK and KHK in a person's biodata.
- The performance of the HEI can be estimated by deployment of knowledge for the three items in the Diagram 8.1. Whenever intrinsic value is to be assigned to knowledge items as in this case, our experience is that fundamentally it is better to look at the involved knowledge either as an investment or as consumption. Recalling the massive investment in any budget towards high salaried knowledge experts and modern equipment, it is practical to consider these items as investments

so that action and future planning are done intelligently. Any investment item like human resource requires allocation of money for continuous training and updating. By the same token, expensive equipment requires timely maintenance to get the maximum out of the investment.

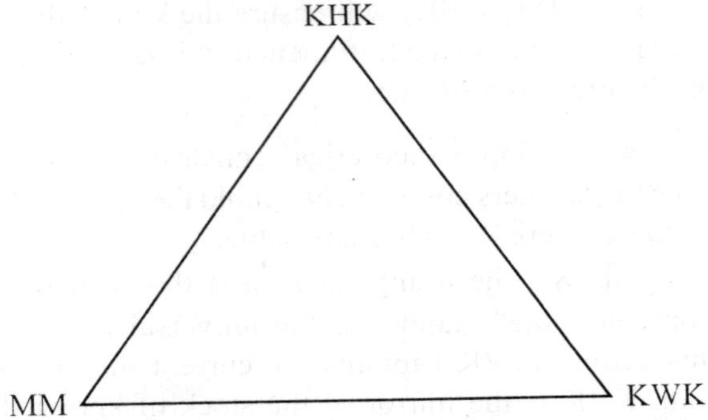

Diagram 8.1: Teacher-initiated knowledge activity

9

Discourse on Knowledge

(1) Prelude

(a) *Meaning of Knowledge*

- Word knowledge connotes both: (i) abstract concepts and (ii) concrete reality.
  - awareness/cognition obtained of passive observation.
  - existential and active. Tool to act upon the word.
- Philosophers speculated and sought knowledge for more wisdom. Science (advent) for some means quest to understand world. Fortunately knowledge of philosophy and knowledge of science are largely accepted as the same thing.
- Information revolution tackled and obtained a continuum, DW. (Diagram 9.2).

(b) *Types of Knowledge*

- Revealed, acquired (scientific method of search). Faith *vs*. Method. Opaque *vs*. Transparent.
- To acquire, must qualify. Prior preparation, pre-requisite as in education there is admission requirement.
- Revealed knowledge left with misgiving. Fake or beyond Science. Intuitive, check and balance.
- Substantive, operative (associated with source) know-what and know-how.

(c) *Sources of Knowledge*

- Pure reasoning, intuition, experience, experiment (Lab experiment, Thought Experiment, Natural Experiment) proactive, S & T in action.
- Specialized persons, knowledge institutions, knowledge

industry, university, etc.

- In knowledge in action (application of knowledge).

(d) Modes of Learning

- There are three often-used modes. One extreme, is autonomous learning, which is what a child learns in mother's lap? There is no procedural system, which can tackle and quantify this knowledge. However, the efficiency of this knowledge assimilation qualitatively appears to be highest.
- The other extreme would be institutional learning, which itself manifests in two forms, like for teacher-intervening and teacher non-intervening (Chapter 6). The first is the most prevalent and is extensively researched upon. Hence, most generalizations achieved in this book take this category as extent. The second is really tailor-made for senior students or scholars with advance standing. Such students accelerate their pace of learning through a dose of self-learning. This can improve overall efficiency in some Higher Education Institution, as in the case of classic distance learning, Research University, etc. Thus we are permitted to coin a third mode of applicability, called self-learning.
- To complete the enunciation of the process it is important to appreciate that no institutional form of learning or its amendment can be delivered without teachers, who possess knowledge more than that of the taught.

(e) Manifestation of Knowledge

- Normally knowledge is dormant and not recognizable. It is only when knowledge is in action or in production associated with a purpose that the observer sees the operation that becomes associated with knowledge and action. There is an empowering activity with knowledge, as much as it is in technology. For instance, one telephone is decorative. Only two telephones can give a fax effect to create a network. Likewise, only more than one computer can create an Internet. On the educational front it is well known that a single Higher Education Institution is ineffective. Only when augmented by more than one Higher Education Institution, the import is felt. Similarly, one Ph.D. is hardly noticed. It is only when more than one Ph.D. is produced, university assumes a new character.

- The tabular presentation below may be consulted:

(f) Linkages that Knowledge Establishes

(i) Industry (Knowledge in Production)	* goods/products (Manufacturing) * Service (Intangible) * Knowledge (Empowerment obtained. Not goods or services). A third category
(ii) Process (Knowledge in action)	* Transmission (Teaching) * Creation (Research) * Codification (Writing & Publishing) * Preservation (Library) * Application (R & D) * Distribution (Delivery) * Assimilation (Learning or acquisition) * Knowledge of itself. Sharing knowledge (Consultancy) * Transfer (when knowledge is embodied in a Technology).
• Generalization :	Knowledge of 'X' on 'X' to act more intelligently and wisely on 'X'.

(2) Popular Images of Higher Education

- It is education at the post-secondary level and it is State subsidized in non-profit colleges.
- Education is really acquisition of knowledge by going to a college and studying for a degree.
- While experts decide what is to be learnt, somehow, fundamental applications and tools of thinking form part of the requirement of the course.
- Knowledge is power to act more intelligently on problems.
- Thus, knowledge gives an extra advantage to job seekers.
- Folklore and imaginative literature always have an impression that pursuit of Higher Education is a smart thing to do.

- The syllabus also has a variety of subjects that are said to be inter-related to orient the final outcome, to suit both the world of studies (WOS) and the world of work (WOW).
- Some intelligent people notice that the list of courses is not necessarily permanent over time. The ideal thing would be to coin and maintain the word knowledge, which stands for any subject anywhere and at any time.

(3) Development and Use of the Knowledge Metaphor

- Our objective is to present the philosophical discussion of knowledge to the level of a practical engineer who can feel comfortable. The purpose is to yield entities, which could be molded at will. More knowledge idioms we use to describe the system more we stay in its epistemological origin. This will liberate the system from many avoidable detours.
- Recent business discussion recommends knowledge management as a means of improving business activity. Thus, the term knowledge has permeated into business circles. But distinction between knowledge and the other has been fuzzy.
- From the dawn of civilization, philosophers speculated on what they called knowledge. They formulated methods to gain knowledge for acquiring further knowledge, so that knowledgeable persons could act more wisely in the world.
- The advent of modern science gave its own slant on knowledge. Fortunately, the philosophers and the scientists agreed to a single metaphoric meaning for the word knowledge. Our purpose, therefore, would be served by choosing scientific knowledge for all discussions on Higher Education.
- Science and technology fused into a single entity called S&T activities.
- The University system fully endorsed this metaphor. In fact, the purpose of a university was said to be now "the pursuit of excellence in knowledge" to add to the body of objective knowledge and to adopt curricula to lend power to those who pursue University studies, consisting of disciplines of knowledge.
- A whole set of differentiation between knowledge and

knowledge was made. The knowledge which modern science yielded came to be called Substantive Knowledge, and became the fountainhead for determining courses of studies and pursuit of university degrees. The knowledge that came through technology and practice came to be known as Operative Knowledge. We treat knowledge as an umbrella term to include all skills — manual or mental. Diagram 9.1 may be consulted.

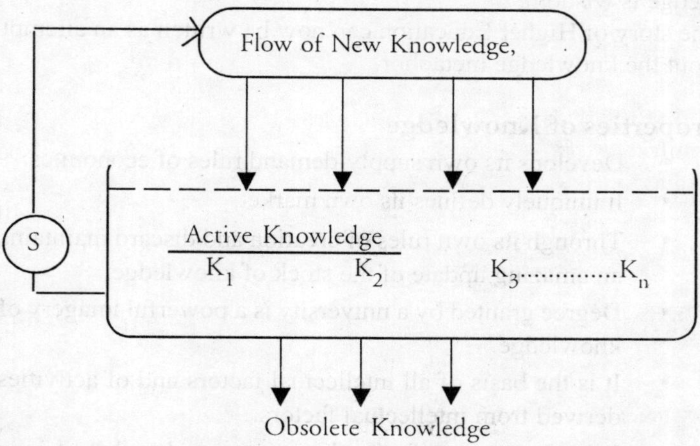

Diagram 9.1: Repository of Knowledge and its Constant Updating

The digital age also coined many expressions, which impacted on our familiar terms like wisdom and knowledge. Computer activities gave us the two words, *viz.*, data and information. These four terms we put in a formulation as in Diagram 9.2. The compact value stream is to be understood in the presentation given below:

W	Wisdom	-	Qualified to render consultancy in knowledge.
K	Knowledge	-	Certified as practitioner of knowledge.
I	Information	-	Engaged in para-knowledge activities.
D	Data	-	Engaged in para-knowledge activities.

Diagram 9.2: D-W Continuum

From here on we will measure many knowledge related factors through the ladder presented above and make qualitative judgements on the basis of the location on that ladder to which an activity has reached.

It is important to clarify that, a mere number without meaning is data: data in a network is information; information in a system aggregates into knowledge and the emergent quality of a system of knowledge is wisdom.

The story of Higher Education can now be written as an attempt to fill out the knowledge metaphor.

(4) Properties of Knowledge

- Develops its own supply-demand rules of economics.
- It uniquely defines its own market.
- Through its own rules of creation and discard maintains an amazing update of the stock of knowledge.
- Degree granted by a university is a powerful imagery of knowledge.
- It is the basis of all intellectual factors and of activities derived from intellectual factors.
- It is always manifest and important only when it is in action or is flowing from one state to another in the D-W Continuum as in the case of the driving force in electrical, mechanical, chemical engineering etc.
- Knowledge is inexhaustible. It is neither destroyed nor created in the conventional sense of balancing loss with gain. Basically the entire stock of knowledge is constantly undergoing change for the internal proportionality between one form and another. It is described only in a known situation.
- When knowledge is free it has no meaning such as in the conventional sense of a free lunch. The practitioner has to put in his own input in order to qualify to use knowledge and gain from it. Alternately, it is said that the practitioner who neglects to use knowledge or messes it up pays a severe price.

- Knowledge invariably created its own linkages through a chain of reciprocal relations. Knowledge is capable of forming linkages. Thus, the quantity of the dose of knowledge given or obtained can never measure the outcome, unless the mode of dealing with knowledge is in harmony with the intellectual dimension on which knowledge is being operated.
- Knowledge cannot be gifted. It has to be acquired by a properly informed person who has fulfilled the educational prerequisite if it is education we are talking about. By the same token education cannot be purchased.
- All knowledge is equal in importance. Unfortunately, end-users assign no epistemological values and differentiate one knowledge from another by what the market pays. By the same token no knowledge institution is inferior or superior to another.
- Knowledge has attributes of a living entity. It has a distributed system and as if by an invisible hand contains all small dynamic sub-systems, which converge to give unprecedented capability to knowledge.
- Technology can generate knowledge, but by itself, it is not knowledge in this definition.
- Knowledge can be described as a big web that extends out to include all that is outside the system as well as all that is inside the system. Therefore, in dealing with knowledge, our difficulty is to define the relationship between the knowledge we are talking about and the players who play a role. In fact, it is very difficult occasionally to distinguish between a customer and an employee in a knowledge institute, such as a university.
- The knowledge system is open-ended so that it never operates on a zero sum basis. What existed and what came both co-exist until the obsolete has been weeded out. Therefore, what remains is always up-to-date knowledge.

(5) Measurement of Knowledge

- There cannot be an agreed method of measuring such an abstract entity. Nevertheless, as practical engineers we have to differentiate between one knowledge and another.
- At least while dealing with curricular design and operation, we can pronounce the quantity of knowledge in a course by referring to the credit hours assigned to the course. This, of course, is an oversimplification. After all, the subject matter of a course greatly influences our judgement to determine how *knowledge-heavy or knowledge-light* the course really is. By the same token, an entire course of studies leading to a degree can be fragmented in terms of rudimentary knowledge components, as it is now done in terms of fractional credit hours. Investigation is underway to determine how to overcome the current habit of maintaining differences between courses while conceptual abstraction is required as indicated in our theory. Thus the discrete disciplines should all merge into one conceptual discipline.
- Imitating methodologies in thermodynamics, we can assign negative connotations to measure loss of availability of knowledge. Knowledge is absolutely free to the knowledgeable user. The lethargy and loss of memory of the user amounts to loss of time during which the targetted knowledge found an alert end-user.

(6) Universe of Knowledge and Domain of Knowledge Engineering

- We have already described how the key entity called knowledge forms a stock or a pool (Diagram 9.1). This pool, because of the inherent quality of knowledge, is automatically updated and ready for action. Before we elaborate on the theme of "Knowledge in Action", we take a backward glance on dormant knowledge and also knowledge about to go into action. The role of

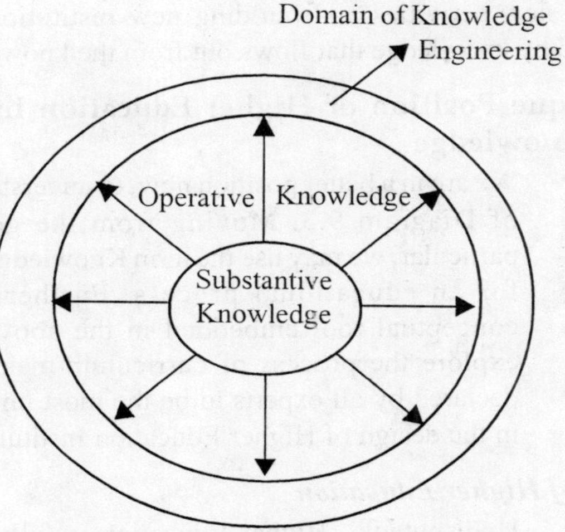

Diagram 9.3 : Universe of Knowledge and Domain of Knowledge Engineering

knowledge engineering manifests itself in an intriguing manner as envisaged in Diagram 9.3.

- Whenever knowledge goes into action the outermost band becomes active and knowledge engineering exerts its control. The band consists of segments of Higher Education, R&D, curriculum design, etc., depending on the way the action moves.
- Let us assume that the diagram is a freeze-shot of all current knowledge, both substantive and operative, poised to go into action. The moment it goes into action knowledge engineering helps the knowledge workers determine the end result of the action. It is a conceptual tool, which is extremely powerful for an imaginative designer (Chapter 5).

(7) Model of a Knowledge Institution

In this book we have followed a system in terms of input/output model. It is implied that, when the system is dormant, we know very little about it. Only when it is in action we put on higher gear the input/output model. The loss of information is compensated by pursuing new activities and building new institutions, which are generated by knowledge that flows out from the knowledge pool.

(8) Unique Position of Higher Education in the World of Knowledge

- We are in a better position now, to understand the import of Diagram 9.3. Moving from the general to the particular, we may use the term Knowledge Engineering for an educational process. Further, we use the conceptual tool embedded in the above diagram to explore the process of curriculum-making, which is declared by all experts to be the most important matter in the design of Higher Education Institutions.

Theory of Higher Education

- Undisputedly, Higher Education is fully dedicated to knowledge activities, where knowledge is transmitted from the teacher to the learner (Chapter 3). Every Higher Education Institution has to at least teach, whereas a research institution is not obliged to do so.
- The available literature on the theory of Higher Education is inadequate, because it has generally dealt with only the description of the social theory of Higher Education and the economics of Higher Education. The epistemological studies in Higher Education have remained confined to the cognitive science of learning or pedagogic findings of methods of teaching. There is, therefore, a major gap. This is particularly unfortunate, because the current dispute or debate on Higher Education revolves around the following points:

i. Curricular relevance
ii. Cost sharing between Society and the Individual
iii. Particulars of the Regulatory Mechanism
iv. Semantic battles around words such as "private institution", "accreditation across the board", and "incongruence between curriculum and degree nomenclature", etc.
v. Use of technology in the mode of delivery of education.

Quite clearly, Higher Education needs a coherent theory. This book is one example of practical educators in quest of an engineering solution.

(9) Differentness of Higher Education

The supreme form of Higher Education is the university. The pedestrian form is almost any of the post-secondary institutions of training and learning (Chapter 6). The different variants are based on economic considerations of investment/return ratios. On the epistemological front Higher Education is in the company of all knowledge institutions and even manufacturing industries, which depend on high technology. Through the analysis of knowledge in action, it has been already established how Higher Education is uniquely different from all other knowledge activities and industries. In this case, the difference is due to the knowledge in transmission, an activity as old as man's civilization. It is to be noted also that by competence and convention, Higher Education has taken under its wing every conceivable activity of knowledge. The significance of Diagram 9.3 impacts on us once more. The invention of a new concept called knowledge engineering has immensely helped further the reasoning process. We have discussed and amplified on this in Chapter 3.

(10) Place of Higher Education in the History

Drawing our attention to the origin of the modern university in Europe, we are struck by the simplicity of Cardinal Newman's description of a university. He defined it as just a "universal idea", which is to be filled up according to the perception of a candidate university anywhere in the world. It is remarkable that, the configurations are so alike between different universities. Perhaps the recovery of Higher Education would take place by touching base with this idea of a university. The university as the highest form of Higher Education Institution is mandated by society to be the exclusive organization for awarding degrees. These degrees are used widely as job-filters by a job aspirant. It is significant that, recently, business globally has given a call for acquisition of higher degrees as a means of increasing knowledge productivity.

(11) Analysis of any Higher Education system

- Higher Education strongly needs a theory. Today, it has been depending on makeshift and adhoc means of analysis and operation.
- Sufficient research and investigation have been made recently to offer a practical and intelligent theory. Essentially, this theory endorses the three-legged existence of Higher Education where the legs are epistemological, societal and economic.
- The theory restores Higher Education to its main task of pursuit of knowledge and all issues related directly to knowledge. As in any man-made system, our theory also introduces the required component of social and economic factors to fulfil the requirements of the three-legged existence of Higher Education.
- But every detail and description is given in the metaphor of knowledge. This metaphor has also sought complete standardization of terms and expressions to define the system (Glossary).
- The primary mode of analysis has been that of the systems approach. We have also developed an epistemological model described in the logical framework of input/output (Chapter 3).
- The Model is neutral to the origin of a particular physical manifestation of a particular emphasis that social preferences or economic/market needs would require.
- In order to appreciate the features of the model fully we have to refer to Diagram 3.1.
- Any theory is putative and requires confirmation or rejection through experience of operation of the theory in hand. It is important to note the following conclusions:
  - (i) The model covers any Higher Education system irrespective of whether it is traditional, conventional, profit-making, training industry, prestigious or modest Degree Provider (DP), even Non-Degree-Provider (NDP) etc.
  - (ii) The Model incidentally includes all pertinent details of a Knowledge Intensive Organizations (KIO) like R&D, S&T, hospital, bank, etc.

(iii) Thus, we are able to place the knowledge metaphor in a whole range of organizations where knowledge is an action through transmission, creation etc.

(iv) All knowledge is equally valid and equally important, provided the knowledge pool can be intelligently directed to the declared objective, whether of teaching or of functioning more efficiently or for using knowledge to achieve the competitive advantage.

(v) In these circumstances, the traditional designs or let us say Higher Education Institution has been liberated from the old fashioned normative approach to an approach which is in the designer's own control. Truly, knowledge now liberates the knowledge worker and knowledge practitioners from mundane existence to that of creativity, a transition that knowledge is demanding from every society.

(vi) The fact that our model has arrived historically in a manner that makes it equally comfortable to deal with both Higher Education Institution and Knowledge Institution, may cause certain confusion. For practical purposes one needs to differentiate between a function where knowledge is transmitted (taught) and where knowledge is only in action (or operation research only and not teaching).

(vii) To maintain the differentiating meaning we are describing the first knowledge above as a content which is equivalent to a curriculum KWK that needs to be transmitted in the teaching process, and the second knowledge as a means or enabling knowledge (KHK) driving the content across the teaching-learning process. Unfortunately, many researchers and analysts do not make this distinction and therefore their conclusions are necessarily not free from doubt.

(viii) Finally, in the book it is intended to consult many case examples and studies to hopefully conclude how Higher Education Institution has acquired the unique position where some of the findings in simple matters like productivity, profitability etc., have gone through a sea change of operations.

(12) Consolidated List of Principles

Our sustained probe in the working of at least three institutions led us to identify certain basic principles, which empirically make up for knowledge engineering. We expect to develop these to augment the theory of Higher Education that we have expounded in this book.

(i) The customer is in perpetual need of Higher Education.

(ii) Teachers are perpetually available.

(iii) The market is infinitely stretchable. In fact, Higher Education defines its own market.

(iv) There is no competitor in the conventional sense.

(v) The market is segmented; there is always stratification, vertical or horizontal. Thus a lot of differentiation is possible in the design.

(vi) There will be chaotic changes and the only escape will be through orchestration of the core and specialized courses through intelligent reform of the system.

(vii) Early introduction of specialization prevents the attempt to come back for higher courses. Early specialization also thwarts learning ability.

(viii) With the breakthrough in technological delivery systems and the spiraling aspiration of the middle class at the higher level, there will be more scope for distance learning and for unusual combinations of institutional and autonomous learning.

(ix) Every organization has to become a learning organization. The junior members of the staff will find it important, therefore, to demand that all internal training must lead to the acquisition of a degree without interruption of family life.

(x) The apprenticeship method has many limitations in the context of explosion of knowledge. In a situation where technology is changing and ideas are changing in mind boggling ways, self-learning becomes important.

(13) Examining the Health of the System

(i) Routine check-up should be done by posing questions and answers against the backdrop of the above principles.

(ii) Feel-good test of knowledge in action and use by rough mapping of the knowledge landscape, checking its definition and productivity level.

(iii) Ensuring that the functional properties of knowledge are not masqueraded. Ensuring that an upward emphasis in the D-W continuum is maintained (Diagram 9.2)

(iv) Verify consistency of the aspects of knowledge informing the process of present concern.

(v) Ensure consistency in the affiliation of Higher Education Institution to its chosen WOS and WOW.

(vi) All knowledge institutions are stand-alone and sovereign. So are their variants like DP or NDP in their curriculum offerings. Academic Architecture and Regulations to ensure that no network visualized in the theory of Higher Education comes loose.

(14) Educational Design

- Design in matter of education, whether in the formulation of the courses or of the entire academic architecture, is to the practitioners a most delightful experience. It is a pity that unwarranted intrusions of non-academic factors put the academic challenge in the outbox. Authors have taken pains to place a total and balanced perspective by putting knowledge in the proper setting. It is hoped that decisions affecting Higher Education will now be handled by genuine experts who have acquired proven experience in knowledge engineering.
- The master designer has to provide answers to the questions that we have posed in Chapter 5. He has to propose solutions to many implied issues in the knowledge model conceived here. Finally, he has to be ready to go far from his main competence in knowledge engineering and offer aggregated solutions to the various non-academic problems also.

10

Knowledge as Handled by Universities

In the course of centuries, universities have been invited to respond to every manifestation of knowledge. These have been series of gradual orderly steps. Some items below will establish the range and depth to which universities responded.

(i) Keeping in balance substantive knowledge and operative knowledge, universities learnt to maintain the balance between knowledge and skill. Here the earlier work of philosophers of science was guidance.

(ii) The vast territory that can be easily anticipated from Chapter 9 had to be handled with ingenuity. As in the case of science, universities fragmented knowledge, often reassembled the fragments into a new entity, created new synthesis and displayed constant originality in the architecture of knowledge they designed for the eager and critical end-users.

(iii) One development of far reaching consequence has been to create programs of studies leading to degrees. These degrees or credentials or certifications were universally named as Associate, Bachelors, Masters and Doctoral degrees.

(iv) There is nothing fanciful in these hierarchical credentials. Indeed, these are solemn responsibilities and the universities discharge these responsibilities in a unique way. Knowledge has created its own and exemplary market. This market is not at all the market of business, where one manipulates the market at will. The market of Higher Education is strongly analogous to the well-known outcome of the diffusion process of S&T permeating into a society.

(v) Thus, inherently the *Higher Education market* is most easily described by acceptance of kf (Chapter 3) by members of the peer group in the WOS and simultaneously seeking parity in the acceptance of all products of WOS by WOW.

(vi) The universities in updating curriculum demonstrated originality. There are two kinds of forces, which cause the need to amend the curriculum. The first is occasioned by the outcome of knowledge explosion, in general. This is not as frequent as it is claimed to be. But it is in the second event that need for frequency of change of curriculum exists. Every Higher Education Institution has to respond to its particular setting where teaching is imparted for a group of students (Refer to Diagram 3.1 in Chapter 3.) Through cycles of operation, every teacher is intuitively or systematically sharpening his own KHK so that KWK, which is ready to be delivered in the next round of operations, is most up-to-date. In fact, encouraged by prestigious universities, the faculty members write famous textbooks.

(vii) Charged with such wide responsibilities, it is not a wonder that universities also develop new approach to the custodial aspects of knowledge. This and other necessities gave an impetus to codify all knowledge into university devised disciplines of knowledge. For example, degrees and pursuit of excellence were described in terms of areas like history, chemistry, etc. These areas were also those in which practitioners of knowledge specialized. Understandably, the pressure for specialization and the need to assign a quick tag have resulted in highly narrow curriculum. Fortunately, the reverse movement of unification of knowledge have constantly refurbished image of a course of studies by introducing so called inter-disciplinary subjects, for example, biochemistry. All we can say at this stage is that the process is unlikely to ever resolve itself.

(viii) We have reported in Chapter 6 how, while remaining loyal to the ideas of the university, each university has almost followed its own unique way. Yet at the end of the operation, the performance of the university is voluntarily related to the valuation of WOS and WOW. This is a very important finding and helps us devise practical means of social acceptance through country specific accreditation, etc. Should a demand of innovation or novelty require another kind of detailed monitoring of institution performance, Higher Education's own market is equipped to work out these details (Chapter 3).

(ix) Another fundamental observation is strongly indicated. Higher Education serves a society by training and awarding degrees to persons, who seek the degrees. It is often missed that Higher Education offers its own degrees to its own staff and faculty. Thus, the practitioner is required to become both donor as well as beneficiary. This is one way how the system internally, does a valuation of its own product. This is well known mode of faculty development, which is widely practiced.

(x) Incidentally, we are permitted to make a statement that Higher Education has learnt to combine the solemn task of pursuit of knowledge with a pedestrian task of pursuit of degrees. This achieves the twin objective of improving capacity utilization as well as the number of votaries of knowledge. This has intellectually made the university system most complex and challenging. In fact, by constant relation of courses horizontally as well as vertically, all packages of knowledge are being scrutinized.

(xi) Transmission of knowledge for those who seek a degree, is at best a very delicate job. The duration of the POS is one of the specifications of the degree program. No matter how flexible is the system, change cannot be introduced as a breach while the student is enrolled in a program. It is interesting to note that the stages available between the degree programs act as a relaxation period for making changes in the system. A worldwide survey shows this to be of two years.

(xii) While it is admirable the way the universities have responded to impact of knowledge, they seem to have singularly neglected the impact of knowledge on themselves. In other words, does a body of knowledge exist to study and implement university's own mode of management, stability and growth? In this chapter, only events have been reported. Elsewhere, we will discuss the topic in detail.

11
Funding of Higher Education

Funding of Higher Education creates widest attention and seems to generate wildest views. Tonnes have been written on the subject. But it is impossible to sense a direction. Depending on the observer's bias and background we receive action plans from Government bureaucrats, from political practitioners, from social activists, from employing business, from taxpayers and from alumni. If we have to delineate what the universities themselves say about the matter, we conclude that even the university speaks as one of these observers rather than an exclusive knowledge organization.

Let us try to look further into the matter. We pose two questions (i) who owns the University? and (ii) what use is the University? We are afraid there is no rational basis to satisfactorily answer these two questions. University is a unique institution, different from other equally important institutions. But they are not the same. It is futile to perpetually depend upon analogy with other institutions in regard to vital matters affecting the university. It is indeed a movement rather than a mere institution. At stake is human civilization. Thus, the university alone must take up the responsibility to give shape to its vision, purpose and abiding mission. In this book, we have suggested certain fundamentals from the theory of knowledge. In the largest interest of society, university must seize its own agency (Chapter 5).

Before we leave the topic, it will be illuminating to take up two sample cases primarily to demonstrate how a typical university could go about it.

Sample A (A typical Indian University):

- Even those who enjoy high academic visibility on all vital matters must accept what the government wants them to do.

- The very nature of the relationship does not easily permit flowering of KHK.
- Although they are intellectually endowed, they cannot take the risk of working out their own ideas.
- They are unable to integrate knowledge and break out of their isolation. Before they can think of working out means of their own funding, they have to plan a different institution.
- Even amongst those Indian universities, which are outside the financial responsibility of the government, the widest practice is to make a private version of the same old government dispensation.

Sample B (A typical University in U.S.A.):

- Theoretically, it is fully on its own, although it is approved as an educational institution by the government.
- It raises its own funds by tapping any resource, which endorses the mission of the university.

Donations are solicited from alumni, from business corporations, from the agencies of the federal government. In fact, raising of funds is almost a full time activity, which has been perfected over time. Major campaigns are planned out the way business would plan to introduce new products. If business markets its products for maximization of profit, American universities would seem to be marketing their brand name to maximize their prestige.

- One seems to detect how the American universities are giving meanings to the two questions raised above. Could it be that the answer to the first question is: a University is owned by the nation as its dearest possession? To the second question, the answer is more visible from the days of the formation of land grant colleges to the current times. The theme of responsibility and service to the community is part of the American ethos. Throughout American history, American universities have served the nation by continuous application of knowledge in meeting national need. This seems to be the answer American universities give to the world when they claim collectively that they belong to the group named as 'two-third of the great'. What is meant is that if one were to collect a list of great universities in the world today, two-third will be American.

- The important point we wish to make is that the two samples are cultural products of different societies. Sample A would be ill advised to merely copy funding and other fund related affairs of sample B.

12

Deployment of Technology in Higher Education Institutions

University is a social invention. Like any institution, it is affected by backlash of S&T. Further; it is a generator and developer of S&T itself. More than ever before, its role in the field of S&T is recognized and accepted.

It would be begging the question if we speculate how technology is deployed in Higher Education Institutions. To be fully convincing, we refer to the various aspects of knowledge activity and knowledge production where technology is rightly and persistently deployed (Refer to many activities as abstracted in Chapter 9).

However, we are struck by the intriguing paradox that in the discharge of its basic and time-honoured responsibility that is to say, teaching and learning it is stuck at the "talk and chalk" syndrome.

It is more intriguing when we discover that in the train of development of communication technology from printing, radio, and television to Internet, universities have fully and promptly used all of them in coexistence with "talk and chalk". Instead of considering this as a negative factor, one could rightly agree that a university uses only appropriate technology suitable to the tasks on hand.

- Let us now amplify the teaching-learning process. The teacher transmits knowledge and the student assimilates knowledge. We automatically assume that there is a fair deal of success in both the operations and transfer of learning has taken place. What if the teacher is ineffective or the student is inadequate. We must recognize these limits, particularly when we know that scientific theories have not given the final clinching method. In the interim, best way to measure the performance of the process would be to weigh the productivity of knowledge intended to be transferred and absorbed. Thus, the twin burden of evaluation along with teaching makes the task more delicate. All we can pronounce at this stage is that in the production and activity of knowledge one should be careful when a strong human presence is evident. In this case, both the teacher and the student are deeply involved and included. A mere interjection of any technology, clinically detached, cannot improve the productivity of knowledge. At least, this has been the experience of universities for centuries. We should not be misled by the apparent observation in other modes of production, namely, industry and business where an introduction of a technology yields a palpable result.

- Notwithstanding what has been stated above, we notice that responsible Higher Education Institutions are pushing the cause of Internet as a substitute for teachers, library, labs, etc. In difference to this suggestion, we are obliged to recall as in Chapter 3 that the university is the epitome of our knowledge organization. Both tenets of epistemology and sound socio-economic practice should demand highest productivity of knowledge. Proper investment in teachers and facilities can only ensure return for the investment. However, some passing comments on Internet would suffice:
  - (i) As a system, which awards degrees and delivers the courses through the Internet, it is more talked about than practiced.
  - (ii) The trend of growth of number of universities is overwhelmingly in favour of traditional teacher intervening Higher Education Institutions.
  - (iii) The much hyped Corporate Universities or similar institutions remain confined to meeting the in-house training requirements of big corporations.
  - (iv) The Internet emerged as the most attractive way of communication across the university system. It has extended its reach, but has fundamentally undermined the library and the expert knowledge of the teachers.

(v) Many educational planners see a great promise in the Internet. In analogy with fast food outlets they see the Internet as a mode of educational delivery, which is both quick and inexpensive. The matter is so fundamental that we need to spend a little more time on the subject. Let us utilize Diagrams 13.1 and 13.2. Now, McDonald is set up on the strength of prior planning of a product (a food item), which is proposed to be fast as well as cheap. But if someone was to look for a different ambience for the food item, let us say a good restaurant, the fast food joint ceases to exist. Looking from another point of view, the existing educational 'product' has been predesigned to meet the need of the educational market. Now to superimpose the technology of Internet, in the analogy of McDonald, leads to a stalemate. We would like to point out that if the analogy was carried to the stage of information only and not knowledge, as presented in Diagram 9.2; there would be no problem.

(vi) In the glamorous presentation of Internet, we should not miss the great opportunity Internet can give to the operational efficiency of increasingly complex universities. Those who recall will admit that the Internet is excellent in establishing communication between scholars. Similarly, those who were burdened with multifaceted responsibility of running a multiversity would recall that computer and other data processing technology transform the operational efficiency. Similar imaginative adaptation of the Internet should be highly welcome.

(vii) Introduction of any equipment or facilities has a capital cost. All items of capital (both physical as well as human) entail a continuous operating cost. Therefore, Internet or any other manifestation of technology requires investment before anything else. Hence we would like to sound a caution (Chapters 5 and 11).

13

Students as Customers or Making Money in Higher Education

(1) The title of this chapter is deliberately provocative to confront the opposing viewpoints, in which substance is forgotten and it has become merely a semantic battle:

(i) Transmission of values from generation to generation *vs.* transmission of knowledge from donor to recipient. 'Value' — difficult to arrive at an agreed definition. 'Knowledge' — definable in a practical sense. Not merely a philosophical exercise.

(ii) Cost sharing between individual (student) and the State (public funds) can range from full subsidy to no subsidy.

(iii) Raising funds in the market. Extreme example is a proprietary college. 'Making money', 'profit'— words are anathema in educational usage.

(iv) Treating the student nominally as a customer can help improving analysis of operations and introduce efficiency while adhering to eternal principles guiding pursuit of knowledge and scholarship.

(v) Financial issues are intimately inter-linked with educational issues in the context of achievable social goals.

(2) Students have to deal with two discrete modalities in Higher Education Institutions

(i) Educational or Epistemological Modalities:

- Teacher and student form a knowledge team.
- Asymmetry of information between them is minimum in Higher Education.

- Educational process is actually the endeavour to accelerate the rate of reducing this difference or gap.
- Student is an understudy or junior professional in Higher Education. He is both a pupil as well as a teacher in the Higher Education Institution. Paraphernalia of a Graduate School or professional school is built on the promise of this unique professional context that Higher Education has designed.
- Student and teacher are jointly exploring know- what knowledge to separate out know-how knowledge. This is the only creative process for textbook updating.
- In the program of studies, input qualification is the output from a prescribed preparatory educational system. Similarly, the output becomes the input to a still Higher Education system. This relay of valuation, inherent in education, assures of acceptability of the 'product' of Higher Education Institution. This is the 'market' for which Higher Education has to work. Members of this market are WOS and WOW.
- Student is the agent to diffuse knowledge acquired throughout the system.
- Student in Higher Education Institution may have a variety of earlier prior preparation (pronounced or self-acquired). Concept of admission with advanced standing is thus born. But with judicious use of distance learning techniques, both soft as well as hard, delivery of knowledge can be accelerated.
- Higher Education Institution deploys all these devices in the development of junior faculty, who are registered as senior or mature students.

(ii) Societal/Economic/Market Modalities:

- Only universities are permitted to award degrees like Associate, Bachelors, Masters and Doctorate. These credentials are accepted as a measure of knowledge and skill acquired by student and certified by Higher Education Institution. These are hallmarks.

- As an investment, return to individual is highest in Higher Education.
- There is an opportunity cost in Higher Education paid by student by delaying entry in the labour market.
- Must qualify educationally before admission is granted. Mere ability to pay fees is never acceptable.
- If a Higher Education Institution obeys its own 'market' compulsion, it will be happily free from the vagaries of the consumer market.
- Some post-modern universities have boldly seized the knowledge landscape. They are leaders in many aspects of knowledge in action, while they run the universities as an enterprise.

(3) The Difference Identified

- Buying & selling — part of modern life and money economy.
- Customer, provider, competitor — constitute the market as we know.
- Education 'market' is defined only in the sense of peer group acceptability.
- The point will be made when we see the student as a pure consumer of goods and services as against his role as a knowledge seeker.

- When student is a pure consumer, he is viewed as:
  - has money, will pay
  - no prior knowledge or requirement imposed.

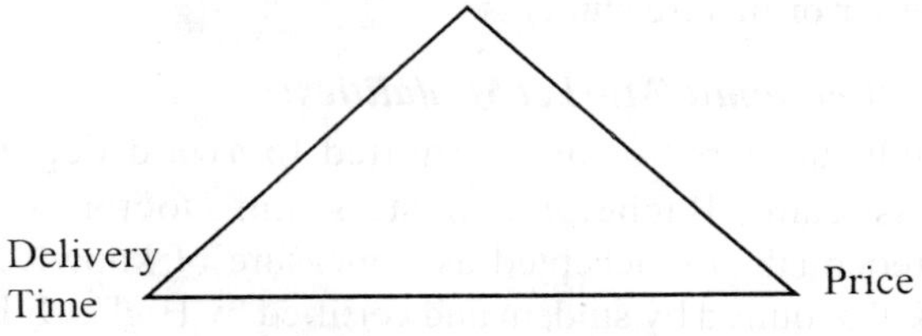

Diagram 13.1: Setting for a Consumer

- When the same person seeks knowledge (degree) or "shops" for a college the situation is presented in Diagram 13.2. He is viewed as:

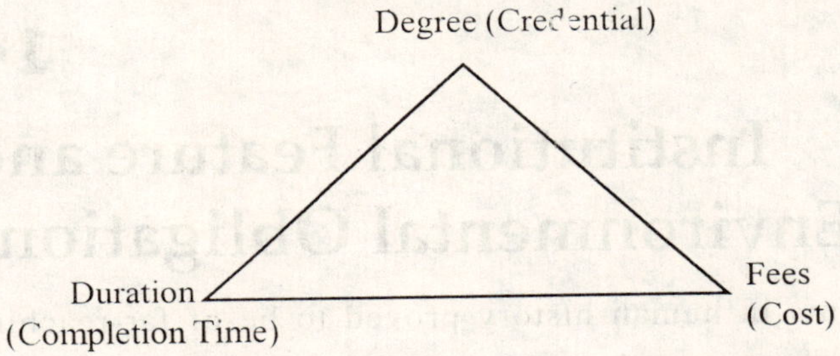

Diagram 13.2: Setting for a Degree Seeker

- has merit, will persevere
- must demonstrate prerequisite before entry
- must fully participate as required during stay in college.

Conclusion

The similarity as well as the dissimilarity between the two diagrams is to be highlighted for the student to become a true customer of Higher Education.

14

Institutional Feature and Environmental Obligations

Two events in human history proved to be of far-reaching consequence.

(i) Spontaneous growth of number of settings of *guru-shishya* (teacher & taught) into institutional forms.

(ii) Coming together of groups of scholars in pursuit of objective studies and investigations.

- The two activities merged into a single movement to give rise to a cornucopia now called a University.
- In course of time, university came to be recognized as the sole institution that involves itself into all aspects of knowledge. In short, it is the knowledge capital of society.
- The environment, outside the system, vaguely saw its importance. It gave subsidy to the system. The basic importance of knowledge to society was endorsed on several counts. But this interest remained peripheral perhaps to the ultimate good of the university.
- Traditionally, a university, while imparting knowledge to a student, formally issued pronouncements on the performance of the student. These are solemn credentials (called degrees) now universally accepted. University, thus is the only educational institution that is mandated to award degrees. These degrees are accepted both by WOS and by WOW.
- Post-modern universities are inclined to offer degree courses even in areas like vocational studies. The

ancient universities taught only the Buddhist clergies. There are no limits on what a university can legitimately undertake.

- The special features which universities have acquired are outcome of conscious thinking on part of society, which forms a larger environment. The Second World War particularly saw the emergence of at least the American Universities as a supreme knowledge endowment of the society.
- The phenomenon of federal grants of mission-oriented research has now become an object of envy (might be called, the MIT envy) in all countries. Some say, these developments have reversed the dependence on money and ideas from extreme independence to at least the partnership with the Government. Some others would even ask for reduction of the subsidy. Some even demand that the permission to award a degree only to universities is only a monopoly and should be amended to include non-university institutions, like business-propelled Higher Education Institutions.
- We do not wish to join a debate either way. All we like to suggest that this tendency of treating the university in a lackadaisical way must be curbed. Throughout this book, we have endeavoured a pragmatic method of dealing with knowledge as a working metaphor and have offered a theory of operation of a university. It is important that we curb our old habits and initiate a new approach.
- It is clear to us that the university as an institution expands into the entire horizon of knowledge. Environment as a beneficiary, must in self-interest support university in its endeavour. From a sad tale of continuous encounter let the two come to join a mission. Perhaps emulating some famous American Universities, some Higher Education Institutions may undertake the task of educating the environment on a modern university.

15

When Knowledge Crosses Borders

(1) Dichotomy Explained

- The words university and knowledge are inseparable. Since university is universal or international, knowledge could not be otherwise.
- Where commodification of knowledge is permitted and acceptable, the word border invokes the politico-economy of knowledge. This is the special thing in the movement of knowledge.
- Better to treat methodologically, movement of goods and services distinct from that of knowledge.

(2) Flow of Goods and Services

(i) Characterized by the productive bases of countries concerned — exporting and importing.

(ii) Determined by producing cost and acceptability of items of trade.

(iii) Market determined by supply-demand issues.

(iv) Basic principles are strongly manifest within country borders. This is the much discussed market economy.

(3) Cross-Border Flow of Knowledge

Diagram 15.1 attempts to identify items of knowledge as below:

(i) *Ideas/concepts*

Truly universal. No barrier can stop its flow. Any direction of flow.

(ii) *Technology*

Embodies the knowledge contents. Ultimately diffuses in

larger society. Any direction.

(iii) *Expert*

Carries and purveys both know what knowledge and know-how knowledge.

Any direction.

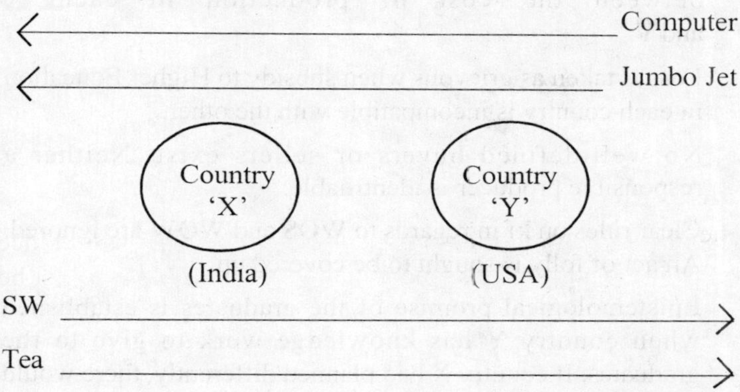

Diagram 15.1: Flow of Goods and Services

(iv) *Graduate/Scholars*

Initial level knowledge workers. Traditionally moving towards fountainhead Higher Education Institution. Only in modern times acquired politico-economic implications. In ancient times scholars undertook arduous and risky travels to establish communications between themselves.

(v) *School-leavers*

Those who prefer to go abroad for undergraduate studies.

(4) Contrasting Nature of the Two Flows (2) and (3)

- A rich literature exists on exchange of scholars and transfer of know-how between countries. Parties actively involved are Higher Education Institution and business.
- The question as to which country is the net gainer has remained unresolved.
- This is not the place for us to join the issue. However, we propose to take up briefly this matter in the context of the theory and model of Higher Education we have proposed in this book.
- Few examples will do.

(i) *Brain Drain*

- Item (3)(iv), when it is only from X to Y, neatly describes the phenomenon.
- Loss to country X is calculated by estimating the difference between the cost of production in each X and Y.
- Loss is taken as grievous when subsidy to Higher Education in each country is incompatible with the other.
- No well-defined buyers or sellers exist. Neither a responsible producer is identifiable.
- Clear rules on kf in regards to WOS and WOW are ignored. An act of folly is sought to be covered up.
- Epistemological promise of the graduates is established when country Y has knowledge work to give to the graduates. If country X had planned differently, there would have been no Brain Drain.
- Considering all flows in section (3) above, Brain Drain or no Brain Drain, country Y is clearly a supplier of knowledge to country X, particularly in respect of KWK.
- To reverse the flow, novel schemes are to be attempted incrementally. When that happens, this flow is more likely to contain KHK rather than KWK.
- It is also possible to manifest in an internal Brain Drain, when the graduate changes his area of studies.

(ii) *Tie-ups*

- Item (3)(v) will represent this and also what is known as twinning arrangement, articulation agreements, etc.
- It is generally a business deal between an NDP in country X and a DP in country Y. It can happen also between DP and NDP within country X.
- Access to a degree that too in an area with hype, is the sole selling point of the deal. Quite often the fact that this may ultimately be more expensive and time-consuming is blurred over. The global acceptability of the degree can never be guaranteed.
- It is established that economics works out to be an

epistemological drag and waste. The concept could have helped the NDP attain the virtual status of a DP at minimum cost.

- What was needed was to aim for maximization of academic prestige rather than maximization of profit.
- NDP seems to be satisfied to act as a broker and supplier of customers to DP.

(5) In Conclusion

- The nature of knowledge once again presents a unique methodology of analysis. Sections (2) and (3) of this Chapter are to be probed in unison.
- Higher Education defines its own market, which would seem to be most appropriate even when Higher Education handles knowledge as a commodity. There is no need to emulate business. On the other hand Higher Education can offer many tips to business in regard to effectiveness, stability, ultimate cost, etc.
- The two examples, cited in this chapter, would appear to be liabilities that Higher Education begets. These are so, because there is no strategy and imagination employed by providers. Just as body shopping was prelude to software industries in all developing countries, Brain Drain and Tie-ups should be stood on their heads. A revisit with worthy knowledge can make country X compete against country Y as also NDP compete against DP if global knowledge market (Higher Education kind and business kind) is fully exploited.

Part III: An Endless Frontier

Wherein we present glimpses of the genesis and ramifications of Higher Education. We give special attention to the university education. Recent events have drawn the attention of scholars on the university system. We do not see it as an evolutionary process, evolving into a 'good' form of a University. We see the situation as an endless frontier where basic character of Higher Education is the core around which change is taking place. In Part III, we shall touch upon some novel development in university education.

16

Rise of Knowledge Tasks

University education as circumscribed by the knowledge metaphor requires that we coin an expression when we respond to knowledge in action. We call these knowledge tasks (Chapter 9). Now, we propose to briefly touch upon the rise of the knowledge task in a variety of ways in the not too distant future. The tasks by themselves are not unique. But the strategies, we suspect will be entrepreneurial response to these tasks.

(a) Research University

The academia is wont to claim it does research along with teaching almost as a cliché. We have explained from fundamental principles how research of the first kind is synergic with teaching. The cliché is associated with research of the second kind. To that extent, we give a different connotation to the much-used word 'Research University'.

Great and big universities, particularly in USA, have elaborated their involvement in research of the second kind. There seems to be persistent strategy, since the Second World War, securing federal grants for sponsored research to meet the budgetary requirement of the universities. The practice is so prevalent that one could safely predict these universities would endorse and further the task of making knowledge as a service and also a business. It is equivalent to stating that some universities will exclusively serve the Ph.D. route of education. The Ph.D. scholars would be asked to do a more enriched curriculum and also form teams under the guidance of professors to meet the deadline of the sponsored research assignment given to the university. In this description, is manifested what we clearly wish to name as a research university. Research universities may come into existence by conversion of teaching universities, which also do massive research. They would also come into existence by a new orientation of giant R&D establishments, which currently have no teaching involvement.

While it is possible for corporate R&D to create a research university, the so-called *corporate universities* are simply another category of Higher Education Institution. They are primarily in-house training set-ups in order to update the corporate knowledge workers. To establish the point fully, let us revert to MM in Chapter 3. Our visualization of a true research university is one, which is planned to make kf as Ph.D. It would be up to the proclivities of the sponsor to decide what it should be.

(b) Global University

The universality of a university is taken as an axiomatic fact. Basic feature is still designed on the knowledge concept as presented in the MM in Chapter 3. It should be clear that the nature of a university could not be altered. The first version of a university subscribed to the universal dimensions of knowledge. On the other hand, the institutions nurtured in the market economy are a part of the globalization of operations. Market economy would induce certain universities to work out mechanism of comfortably dealing with furtherance of knowledge together with material gains for the purpose of educational need. We name such universities as global universities.

Now, the global university will comfortably function as a business as long as it ensures full discharge of its epistemological commitment. Unlike existing universities, global university will talk in the metaphor of the market. For example, it will look upon the student as a customer whose legitimate educational need has to be fulfilled. It will manipulate market forces to obtain maximum return out of its knowledge investment.

Our scenario will not be completed until we visualize that the global university has obtained the charter to award degrees. In such visualization, there would be movement of junior students between one global university and another (Chapter 11). For the benefit of the customer, there will be sharing of resources, ideas and services. Since students will be conditioned by the latest social attitude, we cannot finalize everything that the customer might seek tomorrow. But a network of global universities, together with the network of customers and facilities will achieve maximization of facility utilization. This will also enable the latest skills and practices to be injected in the curriculum.

(c) Knowledge-integrative University

Now that we see a university as an exclusive knowledge activity, it would be interesting to refer to some of the policy shifts universities can make in reference to knowledge deployment. There was a time when narrow specialization was the academic emphasis. Administratively, department-wise handling of discipline of knowledge was prevalent. Problem of the two cultures had to be tackled with the ascendancy of science. Service departments for professional subjects led to restructuring of professional programs of studies. New expressions like core subjects, integrated or foundation curriculum were born. While integration became a part of epistemological need, university administration discovered budgetary advantage of reducing overhead, duplication and cost escalation.

The Knowledge-integrative University is the name we assign to such universities, which go beyond a mere practical advantage. These universities primarily integrate knowledge in order to obtain much greater return from investment of knowledge and thus, their knowledge productivity is far more. They are capable of accumulating know-how, which they sell. They are constantly examining their stock of know-how knowledge. They constantly endeavour to excel in educational consultancy, in writing standard textbooks and new methods of faculty development. Their propensity to become multifaculty is strong. They follow a unique originality in bridging educational linkages with world of work.

We will touch upon few items that such an integrative university (Institute B in Chapter 4) has successfully implemented. It administratively integrated university departments to shed multiple working units for the same task; it made full use of knowledge integration to make the kf highly valued in the educational market. It decided to integrate admission by clearly specifying ki so that a narrowly defined input eliminated much teacher time that was earlier spent on broad input. To cut the long story short, it achieved complete financial self-sufficiency. In a country, where subsidization of Higher Education is axiomatically practiced, this indeed was a bold step requiring much internal innovation and conviction. This is a manifestation of knowledge engineering, which should be a guide to others.

(d) Educational Consultancy or Making Advice Pay

That education needs advice is not disputed in any quarters. But the disagreement is from whom to secure the advice and why should there be a payment to a non-profit organization. We need to remind ourselves that rendering advice on all professional matters like accountancy, law, medicine and engineering, etc., are features of all modern societies. Even when some quarters concede the power of this analogy, they prescribe that only management consultants are the right choice to render this advice.

It is lucky that no decision has been given in any responsible quarters. We wish to point out that there is a long history of bad practice affecting educational consultancy. Almost universally, Higher Education is set up by the country government where the provider wants to play safe and the beneficiary is happy to choose a soft option. In this book, we have examined the matter from so many angles and conclude that the time has come for educational consultancy on payment to be encouraged as a knowledge enterprise. We have provided a theory and a universal description of any Higher Education Institution. The full refrain of our argument is that the matter can be revisited repeatedly through the design methodology we have prescribed in Chapter 5.

Further, those who advice, should be professionally trained and professionally paid at the market price. The importance of the knowledge enterprise is so supreme that any make-do by referring matters to consultants in other fields will never work.

17

Perpetuation of Higher Education as a System

Higher Education is an extraordinary system, which has outlived many man-made systems and seems to be still going strong. We discuss certain unconscious actions taken by Higher Education Institution, which made it perpetuate.

It was necessary for us to first put Higher Education in a self-reliant perspective. Our theory restored Higher Education to its proper framework in which it was born. It was necessary to redefine Higher Education. It is no longer a mere activity at the post-secondary stage. Its identity is even greater than mere teaching and learning. We have established that purely teaching and learning aspect of Higher Education is a part of a wider domain, which is primarily informed on theory of knowledge. We have also narrated how Higher Education through self-involvement and social acceptance participated in all the remaining streams of knowledge in action.

Our study convinces us that much of the epistemological aspects have been covered. We wish we had the time and the opportunity to amalgamate the knowledge activities, which are not purely teaching learning, but are certainly concerns of all universities. While this important matter remains fully un-investigated, we would like to list certain aspects of Higher Education, which make it a perpetuating system. The following list will demonstrate how Higher Education feeds and grows on itself.

(i) It is part of life itself along with food, shelter, etc.

(ii) It tackles the simple theme of combining natural desire to learn with propensity to teach. It has attempted to do no intellectual revolution. But it always provided base to revolutionary thinkers.

(iii) Its target is to become a full member of the world of universities.

(iv) It seeks friendly competition with other Higher Education Institution. In fact, setting up of a new Higher Education Institution, is not threat to any existing Higher Education Institutions. The same cannot be said for the political system, for business or for situations where competition is hostile.

(v) Without making any special effort, it enjoys old school ties or alumni loyalty.

(vi) Throughout history, it has only worked towards a concept of knowledge and allowed individuals to give meaning to this concept according to the person's viewpoint. Thus, Higher Education is free from organizational dispute.

(vii) By stratification of pursuit of studies, through the invention of four tiers of degrees, namely, associates, Bachelors, Masters and Doctorate, it has delineated knowledge territory, which will never shrink.

(viii) By offering options, it designs provisions for lifelong learning.

(ix) It functions by balancing contradictions. In fact, its administrative task is much more astute because it chooses not to eliminate antagonistic contradictions.

(x) Its academic offerings are so structured that any cohort group can be accommodated.

(xi) Viewed from the business metaphor, it achieves the following remarkable feats :

- alumni loyalty raises (funds) on a voluntary basis.
- It is at once addressing the highest intellectual challenge and nurturing skill formation.
- The extra matter of awarding a degree and the value society assigns to the same, has given Higher Education the vantage point. Even critics, who

would ask for organizational improvement of Higher Education, openly accept these degrees as job filters or for promotional need.

(xii) It is a sum total of the above actions which rightly give Higher Education a scope for perpetuating itself.

Glossary

Knowledge in action

Knowledge in action has revealed the basic universality of a whole series of identical engineering-like phenomena. These are: knowledge in transmission (teaching), in generation (research), in codification (book writings), in preservation (stored in library), in application (invention or innovation), in distribution (means of availability), etc. etc.

All knowledge-intensive organisations and activities (Higher Education, E&T, S&T, R&D, Hospital, etc.) are conveniently guided by the same basic theory of operation and functioning.

Degree

It represents the knowledge endowment of a scholar (or knowledge-worker). It is the knowledge capital (brain resource) of a society. Only a university is mandated to award degrees.

Disciplines of Knowledge

The areas on which university awards degrees and has chosen traditionally to call these areas of studies as disciplines of knowledge. Examples are: philosophy, history, computer science, mathematics, etc.

DP/NDP

For effective and unambiguous differentiation of Higher Education Institutions, these terms conveniently identify Degree Providing and Non-Degree Providing status/authority.

Educaion

Its task is to attain the highest level of proficiency in the various branches of knowledge. Education must develop and deliver knowledge.

Knowledge

It is an empowering entity which makes it possible for human to act more intelligently on the environment.

We recall that historically all philosophers were deeply concerned with two terms namely knowledge and wisdom. In that ancient world intelligent persons were conditioned to act within the definition of knowledge and wisdom given by the philosophers. Interestingly enough, when the scientific revolution effervesced, in practical communication the philosophers and scientists had endorsed each other on the concept and meaning they finalised for these two words. This has been our guidance to develop knowledge metaphor in order to explore whether this will be the sound foundation on which higher education can be defined without ambiguity. The word knowledge was able to comfortably deal with the philosophers requirement at one end and the scientists requirements at the forefront of the advent of science. We, therefore, saw the possibility of enlarging the scope of this discussion to use the knowledge metaphor to cover the new domain of higher education as it was able to conveniently do for science. It was at least evident to us that the entity called knowledge which was fully exploited to discuss science in action (refer to the book, *S&T in Action*) would now be resurrected to analyse and understand knowledge and therefore, education.

Knowledge Attributes
It is the means by which all actions and work improve. By constant use knowledge improves its usefulness but is never exhausted. In fact, it follows a reverse principle of economics — the law of increasing return.
It is possible and quite often necessary to seek legitimate means to improve the productivity of knowledge. The stock of knowledge in creative situations always increases.

Technology may produce knowledge but by itself it is not knowledge so that pursuit of merely more technology cannot be substituted for the pursuit of knowledge which empowers.
It represents both the curricular knowledge as well as the expert knowledge driving the curriculum. Simultaneously, a content and a means.

Knowledge Engineering
Codification of right ways to do a particular knowledge task. Knowledge Engineering as the art and science of organized forcing

of epistemological change. As in other engineering, Knowledge Engineering helps deal with knowledge industry. Knowledge-institution, indeed the whole aspect of knowledge enterprise.

Knowledge Industry

It is a new entity we recognise as neither manufacturing industry producing a product nor service industry producing a service.

Knowledge Management

Knowledge is pronounced in this framework to be core entity to improve the organisation which has acquired knowledge. As in many other industries it is not adequate to acquire knowledge but it is important also to know how to deal with the knowledge accumulated across the organisation either as a conscious action or through chance happening.

Knowledge Metaphor

The metaphoric way is to understand the whole domain of human experience and to describe empirically what is normally experienced. Here, by expansion of the scope of this world, we use it to describe, let us say the content of the third year Maths courses. Unaviodably, we also describe the effort and the methodology by which the course is taught and by which the course is learnt. We also call that process as a knowledge process.

Knowledge Worker

A 'worker' whose basic work is to contribute in the domain of knowledge. His productivity is to be measured in a framework other than, say the productivity of an agricultural worker, of an industrial worker, etc, etc.

Measuring Higher Education

Education can be reported by notionally measuring it in terms of degrees acquired. Thus, the measures of a degree, status of education and all related issues can be stated in terms of knowledge.

Knowledge Task and Measurement

It is alternately used as productivity of knowledge in this book. The knowledge metaphor emphasises on the word action and therefore, the outcome of the action requires to be measured if possible. It is interesting that knowledge cannot be measured in the typical way a product is measured. We have already distanced knowledge from a service or a product.

The most convenient and intelligent method of measured kowledge is to assess, even if qualitatively, what has been achieved by the fact that a quantity of knowledge was used to achieve something which could not have been achieved without that knowledge.

This interesting method of measurement gives us the negative side of the campaign. The mind is really curious to know what happens if we do not use knowledge, if we lose something which we are yet to possess and can that loss be measured. Thus, potentially any quantity of knowledge is measurable even qualitatively. Its positive and negative aspects depend on the antecedents as to why the knowledge was used or not used.

Management

Effective and evolving design of an environment, consisting of a human organizaton and a network of material and ideational means, to achieve a perceived goal.

Design

Design establishes and defined solutions and pertinent structure for problems not solved before, or new solutions to problems which have previously been solved in a different way. The ability to design is both a science and an art.

Institution

As set-up for a purpose and is endowed with a coherent cultural pattern. The establishment of unvarying or standard rules of social behaviour.

D-W Continuum

The intimate relationship between data, information knowledge and wisdom makes it possible to pass qualitative judgement on the basis of the location of any knowledge activity on the D-W ladder.

It is important to clarify that a mere number without meaning is data, data in a network is information, information in a system aggregates into knowledge and the emergent quality of a system of knowledge is widsom.

Expert Knowledge

Expert Knowledge is specially defined to describe what a worthy teacher in a university should possess. It is a summation or union of KWW (content) and KHK (means) of transmission of knowledge from teacher to student.

University

A most comprehensive form of higher education institution. Epistemologically stated, it is the most versatile of all knowledge organizations.

Index

T

U